I Love My Grandma

Lada Kratky

Illustrated by José Ortíz

HAMPTON-BROWN BOOKS
MANY CULTURES, MANY LANGUAGES…MANY POSSIBILITIES!™

I love my grandma.

We go together
like the wind and the sky,

like soap and water,

like shirts and pants,

5

like a vase and a flower.

I love my grandma.
And my grandma loves me.